Zoom In on
Natural Disasters

Wildfires

Andrea Rivera

abdopublishing.com

Published by Abdo Zoom™, PO Box 398166, Minneapolis, Minnesota 55439. Copyright © 2018 by Abdo Consulting Group, Inc. International copyrights reserved in all countries. No part of this book may be reproduced in any form without written permission from the publisher. Abdo Zoom™ is a trademark and logo of Abdo Consulting Group, Inc.

Printed in the United States of America, North Mankato, Minnesota
042017
092017

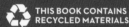

Cover Photo: Bruno Ismael Silva Alves/Shutterstock Images
Interior Photos: Bruno Ismael Silva Alves/Shutterstock Images, 1; Shutterstock Images, 4–5, 8; Stan Rohrer/iStockphoto, 5; Pete Pattavina/iStockphoto, 6–7; David Parsons/iStockphoto, 9; Dmytro Gilitukha/ Shutterstock Images, 10; Stock Photos LV/Shutterstock Images, 11; Vaughn Thompson/iStockphoto, 12–13; iStockphoto, 14–15, 17, 19; Julie Comnick/Ashes to Ashes/2015/wildfire charcoal on paper with charcoal samples, 15; Vladimir Melnikov/Shutterstock Images, 18–19; Jonathan Head/AP Images, 21

Editor: Brienna Rossiter
Series Designer: Madeline Berger
Art Direction: Dorothy Toth

Publisher's Cataloging-in-Publication Data
Names: Rivera, Andrea, author.
Title: Wildfires / by Andrea Rivera.
Description: Minneapolis, MN : Abdo Zoom, 2018. | Series: Natural disasters |
    Includes bibliographical references and index.
Identifiers: LCCN 2017930334 | ISBN 9781532120411 (lib. bdg.) |
    ISBN 9781614797524 (ebook) | ISBN 9781614798088 (Read-to-me ebook)
Subjects: LCSH: Wildfires--Juvenile literature.
Classification: DDC 363.34/9--dc23
LC record available at http://lccn.loc.gov/2017930334

Table of Contents

Science

Wildfires are uncontrolled fires. They burn anything in their path, such as forests, **shrubs**, grass, and houses.

Fires need heat, fuel, and oxygen.

Heat dries the fuel. This makes fuel easier to burn. Heat also warms the air. This helps fires spread.

Firefighters put out wildfires.

Sometimes they use chemicals. They spray the fire. This cools it down. It helps stop the burning.

Fires need a steady supply
of fuel to spread.

Firefighters dig up the ground. This removes the fuel. The fire cannot spread.

Firefighters also start controlled fires. These fires stay small.

Firefighters make sure they do not spread too quickly. Controlled fires burn up fuel. This helps **prevent** wildfires.

Art

Julie Comnick is an artist. She studied wildfires. Then she drew pictures.

She used **charcoal**
from a wildfire to draw.

Math

There are different kinds of wildfires. Brush fires burn fuel less than six feet (1.8 m) tall. Forest fires burn fuel more than six feet (1.8 m) tall.

Wildfires can move quickly.
Some reach speeds of
14 miles per hour (22.5 kmh).

They can spread 28 miles (45 km) in two hours!

- More than four out of five wildfires are caused by people.

- Every year wildfires burn up about 7 million acres (3 million ha) of US land.

- A wildfire burn every three to 25 years can help forests. The fire gives trees more nutrients and space.

- The biggest wildfire in the world was in Indonesia in 1997. It burned 20 million acres (8 million ha) of land.

Glossary

charcoal - a hard, black material made by burning wood. It can be used to draw.

fuel - something that is used to produce heat or energy.

oxygen - a chemical that is part of the air and helps fires burn.

prevent - to stop something from happening.

shrubs - short plants or bushes.

Booklinks

For more information on wildfires, please visit abdobooklinks.com

Learn even more with the Abdo Zoom STEAM database. Check out abdozoom.com for more information.

Index